CW01375951

JARGON BUSTERS

CLIVE GRESSWELL

KFS

NEWTON-LE-WILLOWS

Published in the United Kingdom in 2018
by The Knives Forks And Spoons Press,
51 Pipit Avenue,
Newton-le-Willows,
Merseyside,
WA12 9RG.

ISBN 978-1-912211-04-3

ACKNOWLEDGMENTS:

Some poems in this collection appeared in *Zombie Logic Review* and *London Grip*.

The cover art is 'Cruel Britannia' by Sophie Gresswell. Please visit her website at: www.sophiegresswell.co.uk

LOTTERY FUNDED | Supported using public funding by ARTS COUNCIL ENGLAND

JARGON BUSTERS

'YOUR LOGIC

IS A DOG AND

SO AM I'

– Graffiti on a railway bridge in London's Harrow, circa 1970s.

1.

last night tore grim shrieking words
from the core my best friend's throat
the ambulance his desire
emergency life-blood alphabeted
harpooned twisted & rust-hook verbs
saturated ice pools melted designated gurgles
we skipped bank-note tours
& fled into burning cities huddled
museums of big news corporations swaddled
lay birth to jesus's capitalism immaculate conception
headlines squashed gathering sonnets
reworked into maintenance crews' distant murmurs
the hurtling of

2.

dance of dying verbs
the fact is he is better at it
& they will never
the cops did it
sleeping with the enemy
& the corpse is already rotting
in headlines of decay
while honeybees trace rhythm
chattering his jagged shark teeth
tear into pulpy fruit-flesh
the hollow laughter recorded/played back
no, as if time had moved on
& double-backed
sifting through rubble & burn – the once refused

something here to replace
the gaps in his blackened teeth
swollen tongues ignite the granite giant
flames of enemy language us licking at tortured limbs
mouth-to-mouth one long scream
ejaculates/contorts/

3.

today i sat to write poems but just as my pen was about to hit the page the words were kidnapped by theresa may – for example – on the advice of her generals flown to switzerland and placed in a lead-lined bank safety-deposit box along with some earlier cartoons of the originals.

they were composed from the historical perspective of a corpuscle about to twitch and timed to do so at exactly a microsecond when the vortex imploded dawning ages of an inkblot.

mostly those left were virtual forms, like microbes of thought, sound-bites, and they were busy invading the limbs left over. desperate for osmosis of meaning like dna torn to shreds. shards of the first person singular lay strewn across streets - their logic weaving down drainpipes haunted by redundant nouns.

blistering vicious police-dog metaphors feasted on their brains.
& bloody and ripped corpuscles continued to twitch in a slithering impulse to unify.

4.

exchange, derange, alter, view, war, eclipse, savage, hunter, declare, debase, soundbite, victory, cities, scramble, preamble, negotiate, negate, invert, insert, envelop, castigate, bomb, converse, convert, christianity, white, pleasure, measure, disenfranchised, defenestration, border, disorder, reorder, recorder, justice, plagued, ink, dripped, mind, tricked, oil, define, bounced, cheque, reflect, cause, effect, damage, huddle, hospitals, disabled, demanded, confined, warped, memory, history, troops, grounded, surround, embolden, headlines, blush, sympathisers, marginal, statue, salute, converge, emerge, regroup, parliamentarian, spoke, rope, pulled, trigger, detonate, encapsulate, adverb, noun, riot, applause, paranoid, propaganda, enemy, eyes, lobby, territory, educate, brainwash, denote, remote, demote, class, diamond, penetrate, steel, factory, arm, torso, sell, slaves, home, migrate, punctuate, disengage, starve, network, rework, mix, remix, integrate, infiltrate, papers, photographs, stars, kill, butcher, suture, graph, ignite, chemical, blister, wound, rewind, interrogate, state, monopolise, chill, sunrise, draw, redraw, dress, redress, balanced, maps, outline, determine, nation, proclaim, withdraw, encapsulate, isolate, boundaries, language, bleed, violence, predetermine, pronoun, identity, split, spit, shit, tone, rephrase, geography, granite, gesticulate, anger, pain, puke, book, wisdom, dispute, torture, hitler, dream, market, remake, outline, derive, prescribe, multiply, manufacture, distract, discipline, disciple, copy, paste, viewpoint, alert, compare, write, customize, euthanasia, break, apart, simplistic, annihilation, animation, clinical, appropriate,

5.

ignite imperfections of lines in collapsed **city of music**
& where corpses sang the dead-pan (OK then) chorus
hobnailed defective meanings –
we half-expected you he said compliant with/radio
of course he was asked to leave
thrown against the hearse **& slumped drunk into a taxi**
or it could have equally been
a completely different morning
no-one gives a shit apart from death-ray **sparrows**
kenneth goldsmith as pure concept
& the birds torn
society is drowning in ever-increasing nouns may or may not be a thing
bricked up flats
gentle-nights
fibre
was his being ever established apart from the slight lisp
& the remnants of his ear
bloody & gouged us risky fellows

he told me black was your colour
but the day after newspapers wrote 'black is not a colour.'
my tongue gargled paint – spiting venom – ah godhead fountains again

6.

everything written is a retribution
we coat silver
tongue's acid dripping
& into rust
ears of belonging daughters
alphabets knot/he cuts them into nebular holes in space & time continuums
damage limitations
it could be that he bought a vile umbrella of you
twisted it to target the centre of your eyes
poetics defining fish volumes
swimming like salmon
burning bush visions
striding landscapes beyond his/our thought clamped in a vice
this poem represents representation
those minerals dance an intimate sun of intimidation
collapsing structures in on themselves
as purely academic shrieking designed to delegate
'to be'
coinage in wealth transferred to taxi-cab knowledge
a VAT on words
he remembers the diminishing point when he & all that fall
justice was
encased in a TV vision
& news on a constant loop is a poetry = ripped from his gut

shadows of the printed press
now eat my purple heart – property as concept is a logical consequence of maths' chalk

7.

michael brown lived to a ripe and comfortable old age and died of natural causes. his name was never mentioned in the press. living in poverty he wrote a postcard to the president asking for money but never sent it. it was composed in his margate flat. a picture of goebbels sunbathing on a beach at normandy hangs in the louvre. william blake was a figment of his own imagination. railway sidings never have curves. insert more insert better. dangling participles form part of the rigging on a ship. in 2014 robbie williams, a former member of boy band take that, was the richest musician in a top 20 list of musical millionaires produced by richest lifestyle. richest lifestyle is a magazine composed of words and pictures some of which were stolen from luther's 49 articles and hastily rearranged. poems have structures. logic dictates that there can be no last line to this poem.
insert more insert better.

8.

ah! soul fruit
captures dollars   united states?

tears sweep joy/jargon
wrapped in eternal loops/damnations
pigs' brains

lines interrupt flow
never as good as conception-glue
++=
she loves you yeah yeah yeah
oh delight
a snake of thought
glimpsed   in palms
a book ++ a hand poisoned dart
ooze proclamations/his mental piss

a delayed brothel
amazing example of
as

false identities every headline
trails + trembles
across rain tribunal winds
pavements blister

9.

he slept casually in = your eyes float
burning scars & tramlines
exiting on final trains
that becomes existence (sensual)
thought regurgitates
domination
substitutions in unmeaning
regular pay-packets
unfurl

?

here's the uncontext
stumbled drunkenly into an iron bar
surrounded by vodka & vitriol

xcuse him while he

irrationalises

burden of proof
hawks
disseminate
last orders
survival

10.

a slight dusting
controls his outbursts
his overflow ego + remains
chains & dogma
whistle at his wind
a winding perpendicular
calls wild to unrepentant
doing the knowledge
knowing the knowledge
applying the knowledge
in miraculous mirror readings
minor chattering bites
history's doorstep at **kensal green cemetery**
= no more vernacular
it stops at full stops
(bracketed)
a vile thunder cracks his lisping heart
listen
thump, thump, thump
on a street corner
walking
jailbirds ignite
igneous rocks

11.

he unfurls his = unfamiliar
tense **&** retrograde slim-volumes
targets
drew   +++ yesterday's

familiar representations
his teeth **bite down on shit society**
tongues

laps of gods
launched amid his own mythology
& when they walked into this bar

an irony of secretly unemployed
festers in its absurd representations
hunger & thirst: the vowels

howling dark winds chastity
leprosy
the recording loops

12.

It ... slumbers
his hope of mourning + quest
dances against shuttered lids
pain death life, another deal
portent winds whistles blow hot & cold *around image's room*
lifts the power/his breathing
wain and wax
stereophonic monographs lilt
____________________________new corners/unexplored/ metallic/ cobwebs

it's a turning along **this corridor of power =**
crushing golden bowers
tonight skipped supper amid whisky (drains another drop to feel better as light breaks)
counts his fingers make sure he's real mountains of sighing money collapse into his dreams
or it could be tinkling laughter
a prostitute niece or two

that he is thinking .... £££££
each decision a tribunal landmark
go into the office? don't?
an ambulance (perhaps)

razor blades sharpen
the teeth – his drifting off – his gnarled daytime tongue

another sphere

13.

flights/algebra
walls/graffiti
headspace details
waking/walking/weird mountains
+ your misdemeanours
apposites attract
in splitting atomic decisions
=
crawling microbes detach
retina/red
salvador-style ants
proclaim words' victory
a postage stamp
a postmark
a letter from your friend
torn glass rips
slashes his blood
spaghetti westerns
world of books – toyshops

14.

his trail of ancient skin
crawls across
piano keys

death disquiet
temper heads raised/conquest
he leaves the room tip-toes
                                        on gorillas

lines on his face echo
a disturbing
monograph culled

inside dreams
continue revolting instruments
the eurovision

                                          mists

+ song contest
bland appetite for
flailing words

a paper bag of jarring rhythms
flesh the bleed-shot ear
outside this hotel

motorways dissect

that's reality of urban landscapes
for you
a kind of truth in this vile dust

on the outside step

he tremors in sunshine
walks with a plastic limp
rays of rain/shards glass

temptress's tall buildings
squat across muddy maps
enticing bodily fluid

as

poster-paint iniquity + load his gun
= streamlines his outrage

it's a knitting pattern
pearl 1, stitch 2,

15.

in order of business
off this agenda
time gentlemen for please show politeness at the bar
as in a war to get
action plans

perfection of a lark's chorus
doing it for a lark

we're redistributing
his sense of humour
our jokes –
focused on a wire/a noun
until it burst as into the precision of sheer light
it was the first ever thought and he knew it
a gift death-ray verb to oppositional forces

sunk without trace; into blank
that became a spin-off series/bank station
the whole of the london underground
mother-in-law jokes are a skill demonstrating the importance of music in comedy
apocalypse the importance of being earnest
lenny bruce perhaps & four down
a passionate re-reading

fuck that then got the t-shirt
he sits during his lunch-break at the factory
studying encyclopaedia britannicas
to better himself
meanwhile down the road **they** sharpen
the pointless atmosphere of all-knowledge
since it is the
craven dust particles
could be storms of computerised leprosy
to come he reckons
virus in soul music/
take it on/redistribute its shredding
like him waking from his death for instance
his lute
in flagellation of its own to be
to reach its vile godhead he needs to become
a history of william blake
or in corporate moves/its disharmony
impossibility of zygotes
this poem is inverted
CAPITAL'S queens' head

16.

corpuscle blood bone shattered
concrete
reflection
razor sharp
a mirror
burst ripped scales
trajectories
wonderful injunctions
along lanes purposeful misshapen highway   outer walls
                                                  inner limits
                                                  this crowded city
a possibility that fish will always
he dived
ripples = a drowning = a rebirth = a constant
the vastness + black hole of crowds
he pukes

entrails across – blazing trial
a map torn from
streets his london culled
+ the walls offer up their own violence   & versions of music

17.

delve, shelf, require, desire, burst, open, door, jar, squeeze, disease, sick, ill, pill, swill, pig, fig, cops, distrust, belly, fluff, motion, notion, notation, explanation, write, comb, bald, truth, black, white, stripe, strip, search, broad, church, hail, exhale, morning, mail, letter, better, fatter, slimmer, glimmer, harmonize, lies, cauterize, burn, yearn, live, learn, present, past, future, tense, sensory, implication, extermination, cultural, exchange, european, lean, mean, esteem, enhance, trance, hypnotize, galvanise, party, ties, jealous, eyes, sink, low, pink, glow, mud, bath, joy, laugh, trial, beguile, judge, jury, shot, fury, swear, wear, wig, ligature, literature, dark, smart, replace, headline, news, views, abuse, refuse, redefine, his, mine, yours, daughter, ritual, slaughter, hand, made, old maid, displayed, disintegrate, united, states, big, guns, atomic, kittens, leopard, mittens, misprint, print, section, election, electron, erection, statue, glue, social, hostelry, gathering, smothering, smooth, riot, gear, fear, gas, masks, set, tasks, equation, exclusion, lowest, set, re-let, relent, compensate, state, educate, delineate, order, border, disorder, chaos, supermarket, flow, real, slow, pitch, control, invade, home, tv, audio, visual, chorus, metamorphosis, columbo, mumbo-jumbo, nonsense, sentence, context, reflex, reflect, subject, object, index,

18.

took tiny wounds
sutured knife; deep flesh
fiction/flash
bit into social sore

departing leaving going off
rancid
rhythm 'n' blues

a sad scab forms, encrusting
this was the unpaid electricity bill
figures boiled into stone

why had she not understood
when he said he felt like he was a crab?

you're the light of my life
she said
but then she was hardly perfect
with only the one arm, for example

of course there were other things too
but he could hardly mention those
so soon after ...

she opened the pot noodle
he ran a cold bath

19.

violin feedback tells him
it has to be like ... a mathematical formula
encapsulating equations to do with black holes and cell-divisions
fallout from nebula
gas exchanges
it's like the birds – you know
& wings of gravity
music and wine would be another example
& where the hearse goes at the end of a shift
it's the fact that they can swap dna in a booth
leaking bodily fluids into the chiltern hills
rainwater
the old bones left behind
headlines he tore up & scattered
particles of his rhyming selfhood
slashed from ear to ear
the scar
that's it the scar
is like the birds you know;
& wings

20.

bird is beauty
shred
smash its thinking skull
watch squawks **CASCADE**
its bloody remnants
cuckoo
replace with dictionaries
ripped telephone frames
verbs along the 6.41
tracks traced origins
urinals
rock festivals
village life
a commute into london
replace vagabond interjections
cuckoo
he balances between the weightlessness of juggernauts
highly-strung
an offence against history
buffeted on nuclear metaphor winds
weighed in your sickly scales
short of ...
deemed necessary ...
a line that begins ...
such pure thought settles

eludes
as it transpires it was a fleeting
monument to the moment
all things disassemble
cuckoo

he visited street maps
wednesday early closing
frozen
fell at - **DAWNING**

21.

batter, barge, entourage, negative, charge, enrage, embitter, sticker, badge, sage, outrage, gesticulate, calculate, dispute, astute, turn, alsatian, bark, spark, plug, gargle, dispute, repute, aloof, estranged, combined, refined, defined, embalmed, charmed, disassociate, reclaim, endeavour, honestly, dictator, paper, relate, delete, street, fleet, meeting, elect, eject, prevent, his, counting, mounting, pressure, leisure, measure, depth, breadth, width, fit, split, fusion, confusion, contusion, illusion, mathematician, statistician, government, harlot, prevent, accent, free, speech, ordinarily, cursory, blame, shame, contrary, form, blank, checks, detects, fraud, abroad, word, mouth, enslave, tirade, lamp-shade, live, aid, comically, grotesque, matches, fortunes, cartoons, money, wedge, heart, pump, sump, sludge, grudge, mud, sharks, embarks, remarks, remakes, pulsates, renew, reinvigorate, elongate, stretch, wind, mind, unkind, dark, tunnel, alley, reframe, mundane, relay, race, superior, exclaim, flag, capture, bush, burn, teach, return, victory, stampede,

22.

take this epistle
globular
tool-kit
pasted grey tentacles
stars ejected/variations of speed/darkness
lulled
the knife was held vicariously at her throat
(perhaps) a kind of weird small scream
volleyed into national press paragraphs
photographs/onlookers
wedged between the weight of words
opaque
so dense he could not see
(perhaps there was something to glimpse?)
in the aftermath/afterglow/the lamp
flickers a snuffed life
desperate city dwellers flocked with iPhones
dictating headlines thru pig-troughed mouths
she bled her village life into the gutter
until silence verbs became a final prayer
the fragile sentence fractured
flesh rusted congealed
and the subtlety of her death throes lost
on the press
but the poets ... ah now ... the poets
(shout her name across bitter & twisted landscapes)

23.

1. Discreet
2. Bobby
3. Beat
4. Brass
5. Copper
6. Bribe
7. Coerce
8. Damage
9. Dangerous
10. Knowledge
11. Telephone
12. Authorities
13. Purity

14. Absurdly
15. Factory
16. Open
17. Zygote

24.

they tore apart at licking flames
encased
the lifetime a music-hall joke
modesty fig-leaved naked verbal tremors enhance
dancing regurgitations – the letter **A**

emblazoned her haltering footsteps
climb the ringing stairs her scream subsides
tracing fleet patterns
the courage behind a deputy's shoulders

HE MADE SOME SORT OF A PARTING COMMENT

amazing an audience with his murder
vowel routines
a sleight of capital letters
slithered into the brothel

her brother
escaped
back routes into the rancid ruined city
among the chaos ++ chargrilled insanity

yet another alphabet bleeds into the lake
piss of prosody

fish-hooked for posterity
he raises a bare fist & in the twinkling

25.

jesus it's cold away from the ovens/the rules of the documentary bleed/ worshipping/opening tin cans/the shopping malls signify/rules for the disengaged/we promptly signed our names to the documentation/sealing our love into alleyways/

we promptly signed our names/to the documentation/sent sprawling into/ queues for democracy/queues for the medication/& we polished the sanitised news/jesus the ovens are hot/heat turned up by governments/we're about to explode/trapped in the shopping malls/

& it's sealed with a kiss/the cops fuck us over/& over/no animal rights/no human rights/bedtime stories for children/

26.

beauty is in/the eye/the storm/current enablement draft dodgers/carpet the floor with 100 degree detergents/ice cream salesmen float lazily by/ driftwood/harmony/ she mouths no at me/i am in black & white scenes/on the balcony/dressed as early 20th century icons/we meld/

into question marks/

27.

dissemination cracks at dawn's
new promise genuine
filth erodes from capitalist
jaws darkness/squelches
along the promenade at midnight
   fools' gold folds into sea
   entry into schools/decapitated
   fishmongers cruelly joke
new wave's broken fiends
reporting from credit card union
debasement's brass etchings/

28.

the british love
of aching lawns
stretching out in
suburban paradises
aching to gardeners
the garden cities laze
criss-crossing patterns
in the pools of your
tracing lawns of aching
the british love to ache
for you're in lazy pools
lazy repossessions hint
that under the lazy pools
blood and sinew ache
the garden cities ache
paradises ache the british
love the lazy repossession
tracing lawns of aching
paradises ache under
the british love to garden
blood and sinew ache now
all the lazy repossessions

29.

require, admire, sociable, swim, sink, rethink, element, pulsate, dictate, tizzy, state, relative, culmination, exasperation, shrug, trudge, barrier, scream, realign, religion, stretch, time, nebular, space, retrace, conquer, inner, outer, leader, squadron, hexagon, polygon, shape, muster, maths, equation, money, change, derange, exchange, bliss, bank, kiss, wank, fuck, suck, follow, fellow, foot-soldier, stab, back, paving, crack, lines, blister, brother, sister, exclaim, mark, swallow, dark, light, ignite, fire, pyre, expire, require, obedience, circumstance, cheat, steal, unreal, earth, moon, sun, orbs, reload, explode, implode, kill, skill, entire, history, repeat, replete, fleet, feet, war, score, sore, settlement, punishment, relent, treaty, beauty, testament, resent, product, placement, cinema, screen, obscene, re-enact, advert, buy, try, trauma, black, panther, jazz, singer, chart, parade, displayed, endless, items, choose, brood, win, lose, lock, unlock, sand, rock, timeless, sea, memory, washes, febrile, knots, bland, resend, signal, warrior, thief, borrower, owe, chastity, plasticine, ring, debutante, debate, superiority, minority, expression, deflection, bow, out, transgression, reflect, suspect,

30.

a house
a room
a table
a chair
cans of soup
labels
fred is working on the computer
he's sawing the chair
into quarters
jack is working on the computer
he's decorating the room
little lisa comes into the room
she opens the soup
empties it into a saucepan
turns on the gas
makes the soup
they all eat in silence
except hector
he is outside in the freezing cold working on the computer there
he's fixing drainpipes
they slither against the moss

31.

cracked orbs dazzle
light refracts
it bends his will
the ironing of
his crinkled appearance
doors to other perceptions
swamp lithe creatures
in time; in space
new historical sweeps transpire
lilting tongues
their edges bite into a darkness
between unqualified nouns
punctuated with a dying breath
for good, this dying breath
+ tracing tears
salt on the wind where heaven bled
eyes stumble skyward
rolling in the firmament
flames of his desire
lick at language's imprecision
the new adverts
the same goods
gods flicker between cracks
a temptation to exchange language as money
a visit to the newsagents and then the launderette

filmed by 10 O'clock news shadows
in or out of europe
in or out of focus
the moon maps down its alphabet curse
triggers mammoth tidal waves
swims for his life through television broadcasters
an ultimate goal to swallow =

spit out this poison!

32.

cormorants range across grey skies
they bleed at human temptation
lost to rage/his judgement
first words settled in quicksand
swallowed by earth/deaf motions
a leaf falls
spinning on an axis of soundbites
radio-waves haunt jesus's shadow cast
out the crucifixion where they fell
footprints
an index for your bible is
your justice
shattered like glass in your hotel room
you bend down constantly to sweep away shards
like a horror movie on a loop
the judges and politicians have seen it all before
between courses they are grateful that it happens
mouthfuls/your crying mothers & fathers/your warped babies
however much you hurl
we are crippled by the cormorants
& sinking words in quicksand/biblical epic rages/dust & sand

33.

fragment. fight them. the beach. soldiers solidify straying far from home. buildings exploded. dna. council houses. the estate of david cameron. oxfordshire. the tollpuddle martyrs. placards. an anarchist's badge sown into a leather jacket. the lads are horsing around on a green. company reports. embodiment of christ on his cross. the sex pistols interviewed by bill grundy. in afghanistan. let nature take its course. oxbow lakes flush out geography teachers. somewhere a phonograph plays out. lecturing. perhaps though the irony is. last orders down the pub. seagulls swoop. a devoted and loyal following of the arsenal. and the judge said. defrag. sent them down for a night in the cells to sweat it out. a black and white photograph displayed the suffering of the jews. later in europe. a crushed metaphor for disembodiment. class of a classless society. chalk. first chapter. in iraq. nobody bleeds shards of grass. so he said fuck the. eurovision song contest. an advert for a car. the tottenham riots. in the 16th century. the aeroplanes crash into the towers. paul daniels and the lovely debbie mcgee. the jarrow marchers. the life and natural death of martin mcguiness

34.

escalators
between
frozen teeth
in the malls bitter winds
blow cold
driven to distraction
raise a glass to old boys
trimming their moustaches
barbed quartets
linger on fractured lips
she rests a while by jungle-trees
reciting old advertising jingles
hit parades stuffed full
revolving
a radio blares out across the jungle
they dance oblivious to choice, chance, new links, a chain
always refrain from their dangerous logic he tells her
she puts a finger to her mouth
bites into it
blood seeps red

anthony was climbing the stairs at home. he counted 1,2,3,4. he is 24 now but had done this since he was a child. same house. same stairs. same counting. the wallpaper yellowed over the years. but anthony had not desisted.

a bomb-blast
rocked mall's core to its lurid foundations
ripping soda streams
soap operas/danger
it all flashed past in simulated seconds
terrorism alerts panic on the telly
squid ink blacks out news
a book review lies half-read on the sofa
in the drawing room
something about negation splattered
it's in the blood she said
in the ripped finger-nail
a postman delivers some junk about divination
the pair of them smile
stupidly into blasts of the air conditioning

35.

a quarter past ink – dry blot
hazy sky-debris
passengers on 5.40 – dry blot
comparing colours of their skin
new ways to spend – dry blot
curl tongues shapes of
a shopping list
comparing extra documentaries
black & white
photograph torn off
pictures hang crooked on a wall
he snarls
dry blot
summer is just around the corner she said
sun & moon
dry blot

36. Dedicated to Sean Bonney:

chills meander language lips part-bricked
& IN CAME THE VICEROY
poisoned alleys
so anyway in this book of ours
shadows of the world burst into strings of precision
thought
he emptied
a cesspool mirage/abandoned railway tracks
CRACKS
EXTEND THE REACH
gnarled & knotted riot gestures
the surgeon slipped his knife accidentally
into septic wounds
giants of the warped/dangerous – reply
stream from the mouth of consciousness
we tear at cement
chronicles & whatever happened

37.

where's the hunt/escaping territory/geography masters his cross/mass weight to my feeling/blistering/bleeding/his eyes are tied into the raging masts/wheeling overtures as I pass this to you/barefoot electrodes/my summers/hiss/birds re-educate skywards/dance in the maelstrom/nightmare of jagged history/was this what I meant to say/sometime/I stretch out on meaning-lawns/in my capitalist bathing suit/chatter of teeth bite into the apple/it's the only one/shouts a black & blue robot – give me my money back/we should saunter late tonight along railway sidings/disguised /me as lenin/you as stalin/take the air as pure breath/pure blood rushes to/+ there's another example of televised madness/the bomb blast rocked/limbs/ yesterday was another cause/trembled/hosts with no mercy/I lick at your patrolling of the beach/I am the sea/your desire/crazed outpourings/wasted poetic shells/liberty traces his sand-dune face/cliffs rejoice and echo the his/ our/your/ music/hollowed out/for the very last minute/it captures/fades/ eludes/

38.

counter-blast detonation reassembles infinite/wake in dance
sparks rejuvenate neuro-plastic infamy/destroy
a stretching carrier washes blue chip
inert gasses sinkhole pleasure drastic discourses trodden by sunken histories
tanks & ships & warped planes badger distress
crawling curvature be the letter **C**
dishevelled crafting of centuries
in the caves they collage indexes & melt/new religions
the high-wire of indigenous populations
dawning of sky-clad borders filled to the eaves
new look horizons
speechless forms

39.

where plagued soldiers ovulate & sing-song
abashed among weeds infamy
to tell stranger stories inherited
dust books dishevelled plumage frightening
new regulars distance overhanging vowels
thumb & forefinger trace elopements
a trigger-happy resolution bursts out
ripples circumnavigate
stars squashed into night dust
hunted tinsel sounds a tiny
belonging questions
where this arrow fell
quivering into your habit
fresh on the ground
a flower-study of you grew chased away bitter dregs
a woman's flesh betrayed

40.

lithe in twilit scabbard
dark rose scent
we traverse trapeze
footprints meshed
in circular
nazi regalia
faces implode
meld into re-workings
tears of silent mothers
draw flesh/ flattering thorn
life the only question
death the apposite
walk into my path
turn away
i mark your back
a huge red cross in lipstick

41. Albion Fracture:

i in disassemble
tree/fruit/loin
clothe us money
charter watermark
i
am war-dead ego gore
corpuscle trenches/battle freeze
as acid tongue ripples
clenched in death
stretched skin taut union
hoopla
barter small child holdings
i at we
am lithe winter etchings
a lock
some safe haven
i
the scorn-chortling
dementia bone of liberty
a hacking off
statue stone/face me
i at oh force them then
those who do not glimpse
i ghost shadows
in your homing nightmare

invading force
germ/idea made ripped flesh
chaos frost in ice music
dances i with brother's wolf

42.

false claw eye pluck imprison new precious light
precision gutter guffaw the laughter
smile seductive
generations gesticulate gawping monoliths
raw parades charade pickpocket remain
a clever curse reverts island lathe skills
to no industrial revolution's plot
he crushes diplomacy grins knots
precision enmity hard-core shove it
amnesty crawls last orders possible
bureaucracy battles wrinkles of dust
cobwebs featured empty beer-skin of dark

43.

remap nuclear hospices
crater falls night embalm
twisted hurricanes
fail splendid dancers
money rankles sweet snoring
butter meadows melt
enquire jubilant statues
reconstitute oligarch rapid waves
dead sea ‘em bones
gnarled & knotted requests
blow winds damp fortune
fortunate woman eclipsed
bandages of oppressed
gather shining amulets

44.

a leap of lepers
what's in the tin
it says
on the tin
a request for living
his scissors cut gut strings

avoiding new-fangled dinosaurs

creep night's scorn
in the drawer his liberty
paints a silence always
cherish segments
they in/out different circles
formulating a mathematical
romantic gesture of numbers
we flow
the phrase is this house believes
a pig can become bacon or
some other vegetable
such as

his space oblivion
thought daggers strike from past dream
moon's electric warrior
a full stop

45.

did we create last
decibels order of
this constant shriek
it stinks in the corner
an animal trapped in
its own shit
behave sir

he wonders the lonely
ivory
underground
a guitar strapped to
his belly was a mighty tune
according to the wind
he sought to trace

what anagrams there were!
sifted in the salt resurgence of waves
a chicken-bone of human flesh
ripped apart his tongue

dark-shadow tonsils stripped
so what have we to tell?
fleeting dragons of destiny
modestly – honestly?

46.

let him float needlessly
on the dust of this vacuum
no wind behind
or slaughter above
below only the dead
circling their disharmony
ashen-faced he calls

to birds
come hither

build nests of fondue sets
gather in spirit

corbynite cycling
we glimpse at our ragged clothes
Hull, Newcastle, York, Durham
Stevenage
the beacon of Islington/Hampstead
forever refuting intellectual superiority
burnish these burning bushes
fall of democracy etching out graves
rebuilding vast cages (ecstasy)

47.

resisting standard multiplication
bees in tragic rhythm destiny screaming
hybrid chalk distinguishes
large oblique black
peer eyes/result
grammatical miscalculus
on high seas storms
scuttle mighty ships
rocking in pollution/debris
his honesty catches fires remaining charity
lightning screws an enemy regarded
in disguises of best relations
bring home the tribute battlefield
10p for your doubt

48.

lay sizzle capture darkness
enquire mountains silver hood
danced in apple blossom
renew labour love enemy lust
swallow/tiger bite
its slathering jaws dictate memory jewels
bitter glossary caught at barbiturate time
motion/deep thought
reconsider dust soldiers
& war/torn maps

49.

pleasant harlequins atrophy deny
inspire short relapse
need base october
winter lear discontent
rabid warmongers stitched blood
cauterize dishevelment re-curse
gipsy blandishments hover restating
long coats trail blazing apostrophes
music plays low & soft
in time dogs of europe
in past dogs of europe
spell outraged battlements to fortune
a grubby lute
attire specialist circumstance
pomp and ceremony
bless this house of parliament its constant rocking back & fourth
discolour your tribe
tributes
as if impossible dream heads
saturate an island
a course of beginnings/tablets/ends

50.

resign contemplation hark-back
what came before
a question on purple lips
bartered by inconsolable/divisions/rock music
change returns along alleyways
time bitter locked faultless sky birds
captured/nature's skyways
we translate these tongues
wax & wane
new seminars on hallowed treatises
a standard letter from the taxman
counter-blast to revolutionary topics
a growing lynch-mob/endless forms
dictate
theresa may's ultimate primacy
gouge foodstuffs
enemy regalia
a noun

51.

rose – the tip
desperate quivering
bottled stench of dementia

bitterness – bend
a nightmare of bowing
tread rotting flesh

new blow wind
capture cortisone
rip jagged ice

time inhales
its vinegar
sweet honeyed particle passing time

it's new romance
here on a social balcony
sea-saw slaughter rests on Hollywood bone

52.

incalculable shrieking mocks bitterness
rewind horse atrophy a blade
saddle-up equestrian equidistant land-lock
charming to farmers everywhere
a hearse double-backs lockjaw petulance/darkening out
streamlining nature's cool wind
dynamism parachuted; a battery licks
flames redouble ancient graves
this monument of stone
encircled by cuckoos
nestling among question marks he
feet of clay bricks
hurled at lost jobbing coppers
abandoned in ancient curses the fuckers
pile on agony stop/search/no rest

53.

stray stars darts inoculate nocturnal seething rust
oblivion searched out/cries of debris
hallowed hacking cough/rivers run
to time
a clock in the back of his head
counts the seconds
newly-mentioned cortinas
dance in mid-day suns
sinking below dusk's unkind husk a
melting face hooks graffiti
railway lines dissect firm
accountant-style figurines
pasting popular pastimes to
walls where tories smash
take a hobby – write your poems
we have dictation machines
& machine guns trained at your heads
we bleed your snot & pus
from our arses
wipe you on the papers
feed you to extinction

54.

particles of politicians' promises
blow gipsy wings/gossamer
attacks bloated red-wine gullet
halls decked/grand-father clocks
a winding down/the treadmill
hover new dawn exits
& in came the bodies
fresh meat from war
torn mouthings/posted/painted hauntings
intricate miniature Hogarth etchings
scrabbling against defiant explanations
raw power digesting anecdotes
fat corporate dressing up – a loop
far-reaching into such dark abysses
we grab at …

55. Dedicated to Keith Jebb:

stars saturate photographs generate explanation defies data
corporate industrialisation knives recapitulate the burden
oxbow lakes defenestration paints oblivious matter
resurgence last call obdurate plasticalisation reforms bakelite
nouns the need at point cars' dancing drums pollute straining i
in-sore settling fog me haunts rejuvenation pointless adjective
thumbscrews detonate last sequence bombing questions liquidity
slowly drips language casual reworking workers' cast bricks of mouth
queues statued structured moth mothers flitting backwards between
cheerless orphanages damned rain blackens thickness tubes
no-one circled not once hopes derived bones reformation
torn tongues bite frost tortured from his lucidity

56.

remote jigsaw harmony display
envelopes strategic months banners New Cross
intrinsic wall power artist bleed
badges creep credulous sleeping
lullaby sweetmeats factory horn
emblazon across - fooling jesus
attributes magic trick light-bulbs
to this end
beginnings graze retribution
gaze substitutes
the fact of pickled eggs float
despite beating heart sunlight
& where
on the grassy bank by river
to this end
we spoke in churchyard rhythm
a dalek
passion broke laughter's blood gene
to this end

57.

stand the policy
a document
written leagues blood
ancestry bleached
bones call
this word
a dotted

historical repetition
relaying future tense
take notice questions
dipped in uncurled

knotted guns smoke
a whole continent
disembarks unilateral
energy focus contingency
hopes/dashed
retraining of diplomacy
gentle breeze
later electrical storm

58.

practice debenture half-moon
disclose slowly dissolving
atmosphere of trading
sink set suns – the money

he stutters
half-rhyme
this eclectic urbane
street saturates capitalist domination
a body of his masturbation

draws breath
sometimes the blank
cracks between the chink/cheques
stashed
a news corporation of the delightful
gorges on needs/flesh

take a moment she says
consider your options
the glass eye rolls heavenward
it's only the television stars
& music on the radio

59.

conspiracy dna EWA 654
conclusion synapses
rewind type 6AB
ghost black/coal black
theresa may's godchild
neuronic disasters collapse of
a darkness LAC
strands of her lacquered hair
imploding rhythms/superhighways
it's the history we were taught at school
not to blackmail teachers
sign up to chalked equations
TYPE VC1
a london postcode is important
the biology of the downing street cat
CAT TYPE 1

endless fascination
a pause for headline writers
sandwiches in a canteen
foghorn/the school bell
drift & tundra embellishing
re-workings of her red pen
debates in the yard
offered no democracy

60.

exhale crosswinds chide
tears at gravestones
engrained such names
as dirt direct channel four sport
& other rugby trappings
to claim we were all misled
by statues
status static of the absurd
wired into the tiny sound
our trapped desires dictate a
harmony from the disordered
some breakage of logic from this chaos

phrases dismount a horse
particularly well-placed in the grand national
adverbs bleed
his well-shod shoe
a passage from the bible
floats
into yet another oblivion
someone had said something somewhere
about the nature of snakes

summer slithers into other seasons
news programmes flit past

another bombing
escaped the ever-watchful
fruit of our loins – interviews with experts
journalists interviewing journalists
each a tiny neuron
buried in the nuts & bolts
of the lathe
where what is
breaks the spirit
words distemper holographs
flit shadows
on the autobahn

61.

discourse
this curse
discuss
the wire
a bird
a noun
drown

discourse
discuss
this curse
distrust
all circle – all rust

a tree grows its limbs
the knotted logic of maths
descartes lost in
thought

& if i never was

discourse
this curse
discuss
the sores
his discontent

destroy the algorithm of nouns
adjectives, metaphors, similes
a need to swallow whole this jagged

discourse
this curse
discuss
tongue's rapid fire

62.

deceit springs all everywards
eyes glaze misdoings song
capture natural hurricanes
storms emblazon kickboxing philosophy
philanthropic energy waves snare
drums blown into battle
& on the corners stand
headlines crumpled in dance
amid this chorus of anti-establishment banners
'it's a science' he says

wordsmiths exchanging locks

secrets of men's hearts
liverpool a truck to the docks
a marching band denotes old notes
silver palms a trick the light

fades into chalk disrespect outrage
loops/sheer delight/prisms of dead
along speech pathways golden split
deadhead flowers rise handfingers' heads

63.

enshrined a question beats
heart stone rocks
new waves roar an island
gestures lovingly mocking birds
a talisman reverberates
we found them half-formed

sky enslaved particle's rainbow
cherished outcast shadow's bleed

thrust a polishing of the frame
woodlouse scuttering past
teachers' idle knowledge

64.

gene-pool sacrifice desire
home woods fire kindling circumstance
rejuvenate cattle-herd
some nights the stars
twist in symbiotic dislogic
travelling along multitudes
he asks for
his hands bound to the cross
he bleeds a cupful
his breathing
rust diamonds raise forever
simple hopes of a reunion
tripwires crossover
mountains of wishful
ground swells his pride opinion
new meat for old
always in atomic circles

65.

shambolic destination fulfilled
required bankrupt stock
huge disqualification
mirage requested/denied
asking again for explanation
gross indecency/referendum
the holy ghost slips
among passageway references
golden geometry of index
foreplay forefinger foretold
loose leaf snows a winter-burn
sun-sunk its last hiccup
a cardboard city electric pulse
how he gravely fell
from the tracing of his step

66.

the french king is wise
his followers are loyal
they spread his word
across the channel
& into the bowels of the british
royal family
whose tunnels

horse-riding is a skill in particular
& courtly bearing
women throw themselves at the feet
of the british royal family
who learn all these things from the wise french king
offshore companies/distinguished crowns

a jester turns his back on the world